W9-BKV-968

10.95

The Nature in Close-up Series

Wilson, Ron
Mice—(Nature in close-up)
1. Mice—Pictorial works—Juvenile literature
I. Title   II. Series
599.32'33   QL737.R6

ISBN 0–7136–2388–8

Acknowledgments
Photographs by: John Beach/Wildlife Picture Agency pages 3, 4, 5, 6, 7, 8, 10, 11 (bottom), 12, 13, 14, 15, 16, 17, 18, 19, 20, 22, 23, cover; P. W. Richardson pages 9, 11 (top); Ken Hoy 21, 30.

Published by A & C Black (Publishers) Limited
35 Bedford Row, London WC1R 4JH

First published 1984

© 1984 A & C Black (Publishers) Ltd

All rights reserved. No part of this publication may be reproduced, stored in a retrieval system, or transmitted, in any form or by any means, electronic, mechanical, photocopying, recording or otherwise, without the prior permission of A & C Black (Publishers) Limited.

ISBN 0-7136-2388-8

Filmset by August Filmsetting, Warrington, Cheshire
Printed in Hong Kong by Dai Nippon Printing Co. Ltd

Nature in Close-up

MICE

Ron Wilson

Adam & Charles Black · London

Contents

JUV   QL737 . R6 W63   1984t

Introduction

Have you ever found packets of food in your kitchen which have been nibbled? If so, you might have mice living in your house. Six different species of mice live in Britain and one of them, the house mouse, often lives in buildings.

Mice belong to a large group of mammals, called rodents. Some of the other animals in this group are rats, beavers and hamsters. They are called rodents because they gnaw their food. Rodents don't chew their food like we do. They scrape bits off the food with their sharp front teeth.

Like all mammals, mice are warm blooded. This means that the temperature of their bodies stays the same unless they are ill. Mice are warm to the touch, just like us.

This book will tell you about the house mouse; where it lives, what it eats and how it looks after its young. It will also tell you about pet mice, some of the mice you might see in the countryside and how their lives are different from mice which live in towns.

House mice in the kitchen ▶

THIS LABEL IS REQ

Where the house mouse lives

House mice can live in all sorts of different places;
in a kitchen, a field or an old barn. Some of them
even live in the big refrigerated stores where frozen
meat is kept. These mice make their nests inside the
frozen meat. Whole families of mice can live there,
although the stores are nearly always dark and the
temperature is below freezing point.

If you live in a town, you might see house mice in
parks and gardens or on rubbish dumps. But mice
prefer to live inside where it's warm and there is
plenty of food. They make their nests behind
skirting boards, between layers of bricks, in lofts
and cellars and under floors.

▼House mice often live in barns

Some house mice live outside all year round and make their nests in fields and hedgerows. But many of them go inside for the winter. They often live in and around farms where there is wheat or corn to eat. Mice which live in grain stores can spend their whole lives inside a sack of corn.

Many people think that the house mouse first lived in Asia. The mice were carried to other countries in ships and, later, amongst the cargo in aeroplanes. Now, the house mouse is found all over the world. It manages to survive wherever humans live.

◀ This mouse lives between two layers of bricks

▼ This house mouse lives outside

The mouse's territory

Each house mouse has an area around its home which is called a territory. Any strange mice who try to come into the territory will be driven out.

A mouse marks the edges of its territory with urine. This is what causes the well known 'mousey' smell. If you've ever had mice in your home, you'll know that the smell is very difficult to get rid of. The more you try to get rid of the smell, the more often the mouse will mark its territory. The other clue that mice have been about is the small hard droppings which they leave behind.

▼A house mouse explores a new territory. It will start by going around the edges and then make short trips into the middle

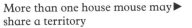
More than one house mouse may ▶
share a territory

Often, one male mouse, several females and their young live together in a family. They share a territory and will drive away any strange mice.

When space is short, several male mice and their families might share a territory. As long as each mouse has the 'right' smell, it will be allowed to stay. But if any strange mice come into the territory there will be a fight. Sometimes, a strange male wins the fight. Then he will attack all the other males. Most of the beaten males will move out. They will look for territories of their own.

7

House mice in close-up

Here are some of the ways you can recognise a house mouse.

The body. A fully grown house mouse weighs about 28–30 g and its body is between 7.5 and 10 cm long. But the mouse has such a muscular body that it can squeeze through a hole which is only about 8 mm wide.

The fur. House mice which live inside have brownish-grey fur on their backs, with paler grey fur on their bellies and sides. House mice which live outside usually have slightly paler fur and white bellies.

The tail is slightly longer than the rest of the body. Most of the tail is bare, but it has rings of scales around it. Mice which live in hot places have longer tails than mice which live in cool places. This is because the mouse can lose a lot of body heat through its tail. A long tail will help to keep the animal cool.

The claws are used for grooming, scratching and scraping. They are also used for climbing, which the mouse does very well. Sometimes the claws are used for fighting, too.

The teeth. Like all rodents, mice have two long curved teeth in their top jaw and two curved teeth in their bottom jaw. These teeth are called incisors. The top two incisors bite into the food. They hold the animal's head steady while the bottom teeth scrape bits off the food. A rodent's teeth carry on growing as long as the animal is alive. If this didn' happen, the teeth would soon be worn away

Senses

Most house mice are nocturnal. This means that they hide during the day and come out when it is dark. House mice which live in very quiet places sometimes come out during the day.

Look at the mouse's eyes. You would expect it to be able to see very well with such big beady eyes. In fact, mice don't have very good eyesight. In daylight, they can only see about 5 cm away from them. At night, they can see even less. But mice can spot sudden movement. This helps them to avoid their enemies. When a mouse is disturbed, it can run away very quickly and silently.

The house mouse can hear and smell very well. Its big ears help it to hear noises which we wouldn't even notice. House mice communicate with each other by squeaking. Some of their squeaks are too high for us to hear. When a female mouse sits on a young one in the nest, the young mouse will let out one of these very high pitched squeaks.

The mouse's whiskers give it an important extra sense. They help the animal to judge distances. When a mouse wants to go through a hole, it puts its whiskers through first. This helps it to tell how wide the hole is.

Do mice eat cheese?

Many people think that mice prefer cheese to any other kind of food. This isn't true. The house mouse's favourite food is seeds, like corn or wheat. It needs to eat about 3 g of food a day. (This would be 70 – 100 grains of wheat.) If it can't find seeds, the house mouse will eat almost anything.

Mice which live indoors feed on biscuits, cake, bread or scraps of left-over food, including cheese. They might even eat candles and soap! Mice which live in cold stores eat frozen meat. They are bigger and fatter than mice which live in houses.

When a mouse lives outside, it will eat whatever it can find. This might be the seeds of wheats and grasses, berries, caterpillars or beetle larvae.

House mice can cause a lot of damage if they visit stores of food or grain. They often nibble more food than they need, and they will gnaw almost anything – cloth, wood and paper as well as food. Mice can also damage food by leaving their droppings or urine on it. This makes the food dirty and unfit to eat.

▼ Mouse droppings

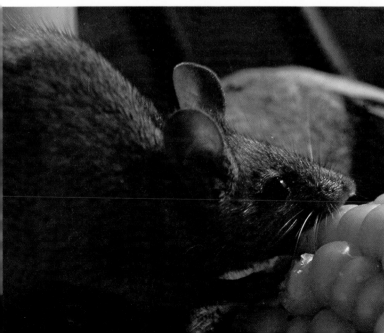

Enemies and defence

House mice which live outside have a lot of enemies. Birds such as owls and hawks will feed on them. Mice are also hunted by mammals such as stoats, weasels and the pet cat. Sometimes, they are even eaten by snakes.

Mice often sense that an enemy is near and manage to run away in time. If a house mouse is disturbed, it may get away by leaping. It can leap quite high and for long distances. The house mouse is also good at climbing. It can't climb slippery surfaces like glass or plastic. But it can grip onto rough surfaces with its claws. House mice can easily climb brick and concrete walls.

Mice can't climb slippery surfaces. ▶
This mouse is using the chain to climb on

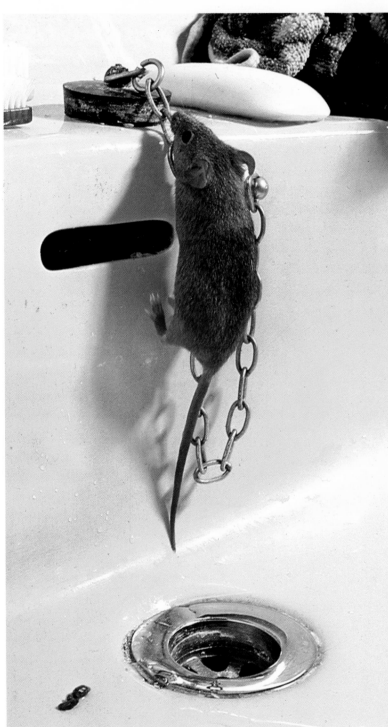

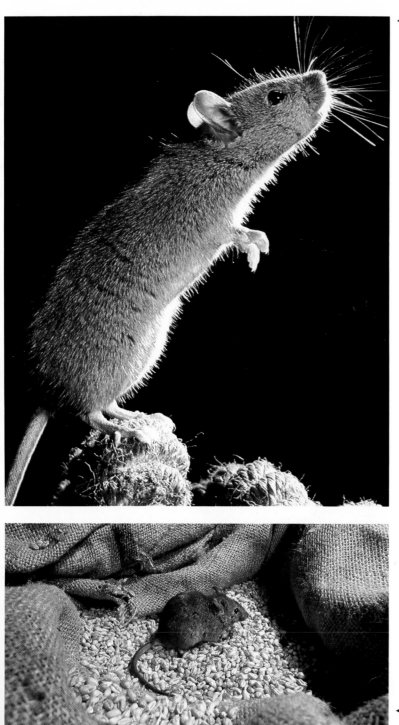

◀House mouse in the fighting position

When a house mouse is going to fight, it takes up a special position. It stands on its back legs and holds its front paws together. With its nose in the air, the mouse looks as if it is saying its prayers. You can sometimes see a mouse in this position when it has been caught by a cat.

Mice which live inside are safe from most wild animals. Their worst enemy is man. Many people think that mice are pests and should be killed. They keep pet cats, put down poison or set traps to kill the mice.

A lot of mice are killed in this way. But the number of mice seems to stay the same. This is because mice are so adaptable. They can live almost anywhere, breed quickly and eat all sorts of different foods.

◀Mice can cause a lot of damage when they live in grain stores

15

Breeding

Young house mice can be born at any time of year. But fewer mice are born in winter. As soon as the house mouse has found a sheltered place close to a food supply, it will be ready to breed.

The female mouse builds a nest from any soft material she can find. Nests built inside are often made from string, paper or sacking. These are torn up into little pieces and made into an untidy looking ball. Nests built outside are made from grass and leaves.

▼ House mice mating

Sometimes, there isn't room for each female to have her own nest, so several mice will share one.

When the female has built her nest, she is ready to mate. The young mice are born about 20 days after mating. Each one weighs about a gram. They are blind, deaf and bald except for their whiskers. Up to eighteen mice can be born at once. This is called a litter.

Mice which live in houses may have up to five litters a year. In grain stores, where there is plenty of food, a female may have 8–10 litters a year. This means that one female could have 180 young in a year! In fact, a typical female has between 9 and 40 young in this time.

◀This mouse has made its nest from the stuffing of an old armchair

▼New born mice in a nest of paper and sacking

Young mice

The young mice spend most of their time asleep. They move around the nest trying to find the warmest spot. Every so often, they wake up to feed. Like other mammals, the mother mouse feeds her young with her own milk. The young mice suck the milk from teats under their mother's body. The mice are so tiny and weak that their mother has to be careful not to squash them.

▲ Seven days old

Although the young mice are born naked, their fur soon starts to grow. At first, it is like silky down. By the time the mice are seven days old, they have quite a lot of fur. They will have their full coat after about fifteen days.

When they are fifteen days old, the mice open their eyes. At eighteen days, they will be ready to make short trips from the nest and start to eat the same kind of food as their parents. It won't be long before they leave the nest. When they are six weeks old, the mice will be ready to mate and have their own young.

Mice which spend most of their time outside will not live for more than about eighteen months. In sheltered places, they may live for up to four years.

▲ New born mice with their mother

These young mice can fend for ▶ themselves

Other types of mice

Here are some different kinds of mice which you might see. Like the house mouse, they are all nocturnal, eat grain and tear up materials for their nests.

Pet mice

You've probably seen these mice before. But did you know that they have been bred from wild mice? There are all sorts of different pet mice, or 'fancy mice' – brown, black, white and combinations of all three colours. But they are all related to wild mice.

▼ Pet mice

Pet mice are quite easy to keep. You will need a small cage, about 40 × 20 × 20 cm. You can buy a metal cage from a pet shop. The cage should have a wheel in it so that your mouse can get enough exercise.

You'll need to give the mouse soft material for bedding and clean out its cage regularly. Don't forget to give your mouse enough food and fresh water. Pet mice like to eat seeds, just like house mice. You can buy mouse food from a pet shop. For a special treat, give your mouse bits of fresh fruit or carrot.

Mice make good pets, but think carefully before you decide to keep one. Make sure you will be able to look after it properly and that someone can look after your mouse if you go away.

▲Yellow-necked mouse

The Yellow-necked Mouse
Length: 250mm approx. (including tail)

You can recognise this mouse by its yellow collar. The yellow-necked mouse lives in woodlands, along the edges of fields, in hedgerows, parks or gardens. This mouse is a very good climber and often climbs high into trees. It eats fruits, seeds, acorns and nuts. In winter, it often takes a store of food inside. It lives in between brickwork, or under the floorboards until the spring.

The Harvest Mouse

Length: 95–135mm approx. (including tail)

This is the smallest mouse in Britain. It's also the only mouse which builds its nest above the ground. The ball-shaped nest is usually made from grass. It is hung about 30–60 cm off the ground between the stems of grasses or rushes.

The St Kilda Mouse

Length: 190mm approx. (including tail)

At one time, a special kind of house mouse, called the St Kilda mouse, lived on the Scottish island of St Kilda. The last people moved off the island in 1930. The St Kilda mouse had been used to taking scraps of left-over food from people. It could not live on anything else, so it died out.

◄Harvest mouse

The Wood Mouse

Length: 155–195mm approx. (including tail)

The wood mouse lives in all sorts of different places. It is common in hedgerows, woods, fields and gardens. It can swim well, too. In winter, the wood mouse may move into buildings. But it will only move inside if there are no house mice already living there.

The wood mouse is also called the long-tailed field mouse because its tail is usually longer than its body. It eats all kinds of different food; spiders and insects, as well as nuts, bulbs and fungi.

Wood mouse ▶

The Common Dormouse

Length: 140mm approx. (including tail)

The common dormouse is now very rare. It's called the dormouse, or 'dozy mouse' because it spends so much of its time asleep. The common dormouse is now protected by law. No-one is allowed to kill it or set traps for it. Without this protection it might die out completely.

You'd be very lucky to see a common dormouse. But now that you know where they live, you could spot most of the other mice in this book. You might even decide to keep your own pet mice. If you do, you'll find out a lot more about them.

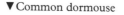
▼ Common dormouse

Index